Zach & Thad Discover the 4 Money Secrets

© 2022 Robert Krumroy

All rights reserved. No portion of this book may be reproduced in any form without permission from the publisher, except as permitted by U.S. copyright law. For permissions contact:

Books@KidsDreamsMatterPublishing.com

Cover art by Evgeniya Khomutskaya

ISBN: 978-1-7366185-0-9

This is a work of fiction. Names, characters, places and incidents either are products of the author's imagination or are used fictitiously. Any resemblance to actual events, locales, or persons, living or dead, is entirely coincidental.

Zach & Thad Di$cover the 4 Money $ecret$

by Robert Krumroy

illustrated and designed by
Evgeniya Khomutskaya and Donna West

It was a Saturday morning. Zach's friend, Thad, had just come over. They were sitting outside on the steps discussing what they were going to do when Zach suggested, "Let's figure out a way to make some money. Then we could buy that new video game we've been talking about."

Zach had just finished his sentence when the neighbor, Mr. Stearns, walked over and asked, "Would you boys like to help me rake some leaves? I have a bunch of them on the front and back yard, and I would be glad to pay you for helping me."

Zach and Thad quickly jumped up, asked their parents for permission and walked with Mr. Stearns across the street. They couldn't believe their good luck, and they were thrilled to help with the leaf raking.

While they were raking leaves, Mr. Stearns asked, "What are you going to do with the money I'm going to pay you when we've finished?"

Zach quickly answered, "We've been wanting to buy a new video game, and we were just talking about how to get the money to pay for it."

Mr. Stearns replied, "Don't you have a lot of video games already?"

Hesitantly, Zach answered, "Well, yes, I do. But I really want this one."

Mr. Stearns responded, "Zach, why don't you begin saving money for something more important, like maybe buying your first car in a few years?"

Thad said, "We don't drive yet, so I guess we're not thinking about having money for a car now."

"Well," Mr. Stearns replied, "Making sure you don't worry in the future is exactly why you save money now. Many people never learn to save money, and they have a hard time getting what they really want or need later in life. Saving money now helps make sure that when you really do need a car, you'll have the money to buy one."

"We can't possibly earn enough money to buy a car, so why bother?" the boys asked.

"Has anyone ever told you the FOUR MONEY SECRETS?" Mr. Stearns asked.

Zach and Thad looked puzzled, so Mr. Stearns started to explain.

"Secret #1 is to always evaluate whether what you are thinking of buying is a WANT or a NEED.

Let me give you an example, and you answer: Is a candy bar a want, or a need?"

Zach quickly responded, "No one really needs a candy bar, so I guess it's not a need. It's a want."

Mr. Stearns remarked, "You're correct. A candy bar is a want. What about a new pair of running shoes?"

Thad said, "Well, it depends. If your old ones are worn out, it's a need."

Mr. Stearns continued, "That's right again. But, remember, if you buy them just because you want the newest look, it's a want."

"What about saving money? Is it a want or a need?" he asked.

Zach and Thad both looked puzzled, so Mr. Stearns continued, "Let me help you out. If people don't save money, what happens when they need to pay for an unexpected car repair or when the television stops working and has to be replaced? Unexpected expenses happen, and that's why saving money is always a need."

"I guess I never thought about saving money as a want or a need, but it makes sense," said Zach. "If you don't save money, you're in trouble when bad stuff happens. So, to take care of that, saving money is a need."

Mr. Stearns replied, "That's exactly right. Saving regularly is a need. What about buying another video game? Is it a want, or a need?"

"Well ... I guess it's not a need, but I would still like to have it," replied Zach.

"That's the point, Zach," Mr. Stearns smiled and said, "Just because we really want something now, doesn't mean getting it is a good choice. I think Secret #2 explains what I mean by that."

Zach quickly said, "OK. Please don't stop. Tell us Secret #2."

Mr. Stearns responded, "Money Secret #2 is EVALUATE THE TRADE-OFF.

Always consider that every purchase has a TRADE-OFF, and spending your money today may prevent you from getting something you want or need even more tomorrow.

Let me explain. In order to have what you want in the future, you have to make a choice to save money and not spend all of it.

Saving is a habit. It's a choice that most financially successful people learned when they were very young. They know that spending money always has a TRADE-OFF, so they think carefully when considering buying something … like another video game. You may be losing the ability to purchase something you need, or want even more, in the future if you're always spending your money as soon as you earn it."

Then Thad asked, "Mr. Stearns, what is Money Secret #3?"

Mr. Stearns responded, "Secret #3 is, **ALWAYS SAVE MONEY IN A BANK OR CREDIT UNION.**

Just like raking leaves requires effort, so does saving money. When you put your money in a bank or credit union, you're not tempted to go to your room and grab what you've worked so hard for and then spend it on something that isn't really that important.

Remember, every dollar you spend today is a trade-off for something you are going to wish you had in the future."

"Mr. Stearns, is it hard to open an account?" Zach asked.

"No. It's easy … and it's usually free. If you're in school, most financial institutions like banks and credit unions, offer you a free savings account. You just have to go there, fill out a form with your name, address and your social security number, and then take your money there whenever you want to make a deposit."

"Well, can I get my money out when I need it?" asked Thad.

Mr. Stearns replied, "You can get money out whenever you want it, but going to the financial institution to get your money gives you time to think about whether the 'trade-off' is worth it. Plus, the bank or credit union pays you interest on the money you leave there. Every month, they will mail you a financial statement, and on it you will see what you deposited each month, how much interest they paid to you, and the total value of your account."

Then Zach asked, "Mr. Stearns, what is Money Secret #4?"

Mr. Stearns replied, "Secret #4 is **STOP MAKING EXCUSES FOR NOT SAVING MONEY.**

Deciding to save money is a personal choice. It's no different from deciding to do your school work. If you choose to not work hard in school, you have fewer opportunities when you graduate.

If you choose to not save money, you may never be able to get the nice things that you want in your future. Whether it is deciding to do your school work or deciding to save money, you can't make excuses without the excuse eventually hurting YOU."

Zach looked at Thad and said, "Maybe we should forget about the video game and make the choice to save our money. We could make it a contest to see who can save the most for a car when we get old enough. Wouldn't that be cool?"

Before Thad could even answer, Mr. Stearns said, "If you both agree to save money in a savings account, I will offer you a bonus. Do you want to hear it?"

Thad asked, "Is it another secret?"

25

Mr. Stearns thought for a minute and then chuckled, "Well, let's call it, "MR. STEARNS' BONUS SECRET!"

Here it is: Every month, if you and Zach show me your savings statement and how much money you put into your account, I will match whatever you each have saved until you're 16 years old and ready to buy a car. That means, if you save $20 a month, I will put in another $20. In 5 years, your account will have $2,400 in it ... plus the interest that the financial institution pays you for keeping your money saved in the account. Then, you can buy a car! You will have worked hard and saved money. That's how you become financially successful."

Zach thought about the FOUR MONEY SECRETS:

1. Determine if what I am going to buy is a WANT or a NEED.

2. Consider the future "TRADE-OFF" before I spend my money.

3. SAVE MONEY in a bank or credit union.

4. STOP MAKING EXCUSES for not saving.

"Hmmmm," Zach said. "I get it. Saving money is a lot like deciding what you want to be when you grow up. If you don't choose to think big, work hard in school, and stop making excuses, you end up with only a few job opportunities ... if any. If you don't choose to save money, you have the same problem."

"You have fewer opportunities to get what you would really like to have," added Thad.

"Absolutely," Mr. Stearns agreed. "So, does that mean that you still want to buy a video game, or are you going to choose to let me double the money you add each month and then buy a car in the future?"

The next day, Mr. Stearns went with Zach and Thad and opened a savings account. Both boys put in the $20 they had earned raking leaves and, sure enough, Mr. Stearns put in another $20 to match their savings, just as he had promised.

On the way home, Zach said, "Mr. Stearns, it feels really good to see the money I saved in my account and to know that I am making my dream happen. I guess it's like applying yourself to your school work. Something good always happens when you follow the examples of other successful people. Working hard in school and saving money really are both personal choices ... and they both make a big difference."

"Thank you, Mr. Stearns."

A "Future Secret" that Can Make You Financially Successful

Just like Mr. Stearns matched Zach and Thad's money that they placed in their savings account, 79% of people work for companies that provide a retirement plan for their workers that matches what they save each month. For instance, if the worker saves $100 per month, the company matches it with another $100. It is FREE money … just like Mr. Stearns gave to Zach and Thad! Don't ever pass up a FREE MONEY MATCH where you work. When you are 21 years old and employed, start saving just $100 per month from your paycheck.

When the company matches your $100 and assuming the retirement plan earns 7% per year, which is paid to your account, in 45 years (retirement time) your account value will be worth $510,584. That's over half a million dollars! However, here is the bad news. If you spend too much when you're young and wait 10 years to begin saving, your account value at retirement will now only be worth $267,443. That's a loss of $243,141, because you spent too much on "wants." Waiting a few years to save is a bad TRADE-OFF! Make a personal choice to save early. Saving money is what highly successful people do. Everyone can become financially successful when they make the choice to think smart, work hard, save money and are determined to make their dreams come true!

THAD'S BISTRO

34

Questions to Answer

35

Questions: 1

1. **Write out Money Secret #1 and describe 4 things that are wants and 4 things that are needs:**

   Money Secret #1 ....

   Wants   **Needs**

   ....
   ....
   ....
   ....

2. **Write out Money Secret #2 and explain why purchasing a video game was a bad trade-off for Zach and Thad.**

   Money Secret #2 ....
   ....
   ....
   ....

3. **Give personal examples of times when you chose to spend money, but now wish you had saved it to purchase something more meaningful. What can you change so it doesn't happen in the future?**

   ....
   ....
   ....

Questions: 2

1. Write out Money Secret #3, then explain why choosing to save money in a bank or credit union is a successful idea.

   Money Secret #3 ....
   ....
   ....
   ....

2. If you put a portion of everything you earned or were given into your savings account throughout the year, explain what you might want to buy someday in the future. ....
   ....
   ....
   ....

3. Money Secret #4, STOP MAKING EXCUSES FOR SAVING MONEY. Explain the following statements:

   a. Not saving money hurts my goal of becoming financially successful: ....
      ....
      ....
      ....

   b. Not working hard in school harms my goal of having a successful future: ....
      ....
      ....
      ....

Questions: 3

1. Review the "Future Secret" at the end of the book and explain why not saving money when you are young and starting your first full-time job can hurt you in the future. ....
   ....
   ....
   ....

2. Share what you think was the most important thing you learned from this book and why it should be important to everyone.
   ....
   ....
   ....
   ....

3. Explain how the saying, "MY CHOICES TODAY DETERMINE MY FUTURE" relate to:

   a. Working hard in school: ....
   ....
   ....
   ....

   b. Saving money: ....
   ....
   ....
   ....

Just For Fun:

Think of a job you would like to do in your neighborhood to make money such as a dog walker or raking leaves. Draw a picture of yourself doing this job and earning money you can save for your future.

What is something important you will need in the future that costs money? Draw a picture of yourself enjoying this thing (like a car or a house) or an activity (such as going to college) that you have saved to buy for yourself.

— THAD MOFFITT —

Success takes sacrifice. Making good grades, performing well on a test, training for a sport, even saving money takes determination and commitment to not get sidetracked. Success starts with DREAMING BIG, but nothing happens unless you work hard and determine to never make an excuse. Just DO IT!

So, as I have committed to being a professional race car driver, I encourage you to commit to your goal. Whether it's to become a police officer, an engineer, a doctor, a nurse, a schoolteacher, or an electrician — accomplish your dream. Be proud. Make your goal a reality.

Success is never given, it's earned. Winning is up to YOU.
Start your engine! The race is on.

Thad

After an impressive first season of full-time ARCA competition, Thad Moffitt clearly shares the same competitive genes that made his grandfather, Richard Petty, the King of NASCAR, the NASCAR Cup Series' all-time wins leader.

The 20-year-old earned his best career ARCA finish of P4 at Memphis International Raceway in September of 2020. In 13 starts that year, he earned three top-five and eight top-10 finishes.